Growing Cannabis Indoors

Grow your Own Marijuana Indoors with this Simple and Easy Guide

Chris Jones

Table of Contents

Interesting Facts about Marijuana and Growing...............5

Chapter 1: The Basics of Growing...................11

Chapter 2: Cannabis Seeds...............................17

Chapter 3: Selecting Lights for the Plants......................20

Chapter 4: Soil and Fertilizer...........................28

Chapter 5: Temperature and Ventilation.......................34

Chapter 6: Watering..37

Chapter 7: Things to Watch Out.........................40

Chapter 8: Pruning the Plants.........................42

Chapter 9: Harvesting and Curing...................48

Conclusion..50

Interesting Facts about Marijuana and Growing

The history of cannabis stretches further back than you may think. There are records of people from thousands of years ago cultivating this useful plant, such as the account from China that dates back to the year 28 B.C. In these specific accounts, people reported using marijuana for medicinal purposes. There was also the case of a mummy found in Egypt which had traces of THC (the psychoactive property of cannabis) on it, dating back at least 3,000 years.

Sativa (one of the strains of cannabis) may just be one of the most recognizable plants in the world. Photos of this particular type of leaf (the popular green leaf that nearly everyone recognizes) appear everywhere from anti-drug books to news outlets to Internet forums. The symbol even frequently appears on clothing. The sativa leaf is featured on bumper stickers, jewelry, and even graffiti or other forms of art. It has an artistically appealing shape to it, with the leaves radiating from the middle quite symmetrically, appearing similar to a hand shape. It's true that most people are aware of what the plant, or at least the individual leaf, looks like, but most aren't aware of how the plant is actually grown or other basic facts about it.

Methods of using Marijuana:

Each time a person ingests marijuana, either by smoking, eating, or some other method, THC enters the body along with other chemical properties of the plant. These chemicals, including the THC, will travel through the user's blood and make their way to the brain, along with the body as a whole. The most recognizable and potent of these chemicals is the THC, which causes the "high" people receive when they ingest marijuana.

The method that the average person is most familiar with for ingesting marijuana is smoking it, which is also the quickest way to get it into your bloodstream. The lungs will absorb, almost instantly after the inhalation, the marijuana smoke. Some users prefer to use vaporizers, which allows for the chemical to be inhaled without actually burning the plant matter.

Marijuana's Effects on the Brain:

When it is smoked, marijuana has the strongest effects within the first couple of hours after inhaling the smoke. Regardless of this short time period, the chemicals of the plant actually remain in your body a lot longer than that. THC has what is referred to as a terminal half life, and it lasts anywhere from one day to about 10 days, taking into consideration how potent the cannabis was and the amount ingested.

The Potency of Cannabis:

It is believed by some that cannabis in present day is a lot stronger than it was a few decades ago, and this subject is debated frequently. The government of the United States claims that modern marijuana is up to 25 times more potent than it was back in the '60s. It is most certainly true that there are a larger amount of strains available today, meaning that stronger marijuana is more common now than it was before.

Interesting Facts about Growing Cannabis:

Having vegetable or flower gardens is an enjoyed pastime of many people, and growing cannabis at home is a pursuit that every enjoyer of marijuana would like to partake in. It's important to always be aware of what the laws are in the areas you live and try your best not to break any rules about growing.

Marijuana is not only useful in a variety of ways, but an extremely interesting plant, in general. People have been aware of this for millennia. Growing your own cannabis at home can be a fun (and busy) process that many people enjoy immensely. This is a commonly known fact, but a lot of people don't know certain facts about the process. Here are some interesting facts about growing cannabis:

- **It can grow nearly anywhere:** One of the reasons this plant has earned the nickname "weed" is because it is insanely adaptive and can survive in many different climates. This, in addition to people having mastered indoor growing means that marijuana can be grown virtually anywhere.

- **Urine (from humans) can be used as cannabis fertilizer:** That's right, human urine contains valuable fertilizing properties. The liquid contains high levels of nitrogen, which cannabis requires to grow. This doesn't mean that you should just start throwing urine directly on your marijuana plants now. If you decide to take advantage of the valuable nutrients available in urine, be sure to dilute it in water first and use it immediately to prevent ammonia from forming. This is probably the cheapest way that you can get extra nutrients into your cannabis.

- **George Washington and Thomas Jefferson grew hemp:** It's unclear whether they actually smoked marijuana or not, but both of these famous men grew it in their yards. This was actually a requirement in the times of the American Revolution. How strange to think that something that is illegal in many places in modern days was required back then.

- **Cannabis can be grown using waste from fish:** Fish will always excrete waste and urine, so why not benefit from it in some way? Something has been invented that has combined hydroponics with aqua farming, and the fish waste ends up having great properties for gardens. The excrement and urine from the fish get transformed into valuable nitrates by certain types of bacteria and end up being used by cannabis plants to aid the growing process of the plants.

- **Marijuana has been shown to fight Alzheimer's:** If you don't want to develop Alzheimer's, you may want to consider growing some weed. THC has been shown to limit the main agent that causes Alzheimer's; brain plaque. The more natural the marijuana is, the better the health benefits. Working on puzzles and playing strategy games is also a great way to prevent Alzheimer's.

- **It isn't uncommon for people to grow marijuana on public property:** It sounds backwards, but this is more common than you think! It's known as guerrilla farming, and can actually be safer than growing weed in your own yard if you live somewhere where it isn't legal. Guerrilla farming usually entails people growing their marijuana in a state or national park, and even though it could be considered more risky than growing indoors, but you can grow it away from prying eyes in an anonymous way.

- **You can grow weed without soil:** Although it's the most common method used, soil is not absolutely necessary for growing cannabis. Using special solutions, it's possible to grow your plants in water, even without fish waste. Hydroponic systems are available that allow the roots to float in water and absorb all the nutrients they need. This innovative system produces high quality marijuana which is equal to plants grown in soil.

- **The sex of the plant can be determined when the seeds first sprout:** Although this trick isn't considered a very scientific one, it works most of the time. When seeds sprout from the side, they tend to be male, while top or bottom sprouting seeds are almost always female. The explanation for this phenomenon is quite unknown, and it doesn't mean that you should throw away seeds that sprout from the sides, but it's an interesting trick to use when you grow.

Chapter 1: The Basics of Growing

Growing indoors is quickly becoming a popular pastime for Americans, especially since the overall attitudes toward the plants and its benefits are changing more and more each day. The reasons why it's becoming so popular are as varied as the strains of weed available nowadays. Many people find marijuana enjoyable, and it isn't as difficult as people believe to grow, which means people are becoming wise to the opportunities this presents.

With the rise of interest and experimenting in regards to cultivating (non-narcotic) plants inside the house, it stands to reason that people would eventually catch on and start growing marijuana as well, using their knowledge of house plants as a base to start from.

Things to keep in mind when considering starting a grow operation:

Many people who enjoy the occasional joint may have a hard time finding a place to get it or deal with other difficulties about society's attitude toward this useful plant. Although attitudes have come a long way, they still have far to go, and the plant gets demonized regularly. In some places, there is the legality aspect to keep in mind, and growing weed at home is highly illegal, just as selling, smoking, or buying it is. It's important to keep these laws in mind, depending on where you live, and act accordingly. One of the greatest reasons for growing marijuana at home is the joy you will get from observing the seeds you selected grow to become the most beautiful house plant of all.

Growing plants indoors can be superior to outdoor operations for a number of reasons. The plants are allowed to grow in supervised conditions without being subject to as many risks as they would outdoors from unforeseen weather conditions, pests, or other mishaps. Once the gardener has the perfect system worked out, indoor operations are a reliable way to produce high quality buds. The main challenge or inconvenience of going this route is dealing with the strong smell that is likely to occur along with the growth operation.

Cannabis for both medicinal and recreational uses is now far beyond only the earth's tropical or warm climates, so for many people who enjoy it, indoor grow setups are the only choice they have. Indoor marijuana growing has never before seen the level of popularity it is at today. It has also never been this simple or easy to grow your own high quality cannabis.

The Internet provides growers with unlimited access to advice, information, suppliers of seeds and equipment, and all the necessary implements to get started on your own garden. Of course, the best plants always come from the best seeds, so make sure you prioritize the quality of those, first and foremost.

One of the best tips for selecting seeds is choosing a variety of types. The quality of the plants you grow and how much you will get from them depends on a variety of factors, when it comes to growing indoors:

- The variety of seeds.

- The temperature and climate of the grow room.

- Whether you're using clones or seeds.

- How long it takes the plants to flower.

In this chapter we will briefly review the necessary implements you need to get started with growing your own indoor marijuana, then get into more detail on each section in the later chapters.

Light:

Growing marijuana inside has become extremely common in the past couple of decades. When it's done right, a quality crop of buds will be provided, which beats what you can find anywhere else. To grow your own weed inside requires that you use artificial lights instead of sunlight, of course. The lights usually take a lot of power and wars to run and are known as high pressure sodium (HPS) lights. You can also use LED light, metal halide, or fluorescent lights with success.

Marijuana is an adaptable plant that can grow in many different environments, but one inescapable aspect of growing is making sure the plants get a lot of light. Any effective indoor operation must prioritize this. 250 watts is the absolute minimum you should opt for, but ideally you will get lights that are two or even three times stronger than that. The more light you have, the larger, denser, and all around better harvests you will enjoy. In addition to delivering strong levels of light, the efficient grower of indoor marijuana knows to have the plants close to the light to make sure they are getting what they need on their buds and leaves. Often growers, either recreational or medical, will have a growing area or at least one to two square meters, below one powerful, high pressure sodium light of anywhere from 400 to 400 watts.

Soil:

Quality indoor rooms for growing let the plants allow the plants plenty of space to grow freely in whatever medium is chosen, but soil is most commonly used for these operations. When marijuana is grown in soil, the plants typically benefit from 25% coco fiber or perlite being included in the soil, which will allow for more quality aeration. But there are a number of other additions you can use to increase the success rate.

Watering:

One mistake that is commonly made my beginner growers is giving plants grown in soil too much water. While growing, you will learn to recognize what weight your plants should be at and know when they could use more water. If you water soil marijuana plants too often, you will not only slow down the flowering process but also get a lower quality and yield from the cannabis plants.

Plant feeds or nutrients for marijuana:

Indoor marijuana growing operations means needing to be educated about plant feeds, which isn't as complicated as it may sound on the surface. All this will do is allow the roots of your plants to receive necessary nutrients and contribute to their overall quality and growth. Whether the roots are growing in a hydroponic system, clay pebbles, or coir, these nutrients are needed. Even plants that are grown in soil must have nutrients added when the soil has been sapped of what nutrients it already delivers naturally.

Make sure you are reading the labels to find nutritional information and don't succumb to the temptation to go above the levels of recommended nutrients for new plants. Newbies want their plants to grow big and strong so often want to add more than enough fertilizer to the plants, but this is not a smart move. More experienced growers eventually learn to observe their plants and know by how they look whether they require additional nutrients or need to be watered.

This book was written with the intention of being easily understandable, even to the layman, and tries not to delve into any gardening or botany techniques that are too advanced for a beginner. After reading this book, the average person should be able to start their own grow operation, even if they knew nothing about how it worked before reading.

Chapter 2: Cannabis Seeds

Anyone can grow cannabis indoors, even if you have never had any experience with it or plants in general. You can start your own garden and enjoy a highly successful harvest by following along closely with the instructions I will give you in this book.

If you have given growing a try before and had trouble, you may discover a solution in the later pages of this book. Of course, the best quality buds will come from the best quality seeds, so the first step is to procure those.

If you don't already have seeds on hand, you will need to either ask around, save seeds out of existing marijuana of a good strain (making sure that they are solid and not hollow), or ordering them online. You may discover that many people have an existing collection of seeds at home and are willing to give some out as long as they get to enjoy some of the harvest when they are done growing. The best thing to do is ask around, and if that doesn't work, look online.

The germination of marijuana seeds is possible through a variety of methods, and the Internet is full of grow forums that get into detailed specifics. In this book, I will cover the simplest and easiest methods you can use.

- Put the seeds into soil, about 1 centimeter deep. By far the simplest method of all is to plant the seeds right away, but there's a chance that some may not come up. The soil should be damp and pressed firmly. A layer of cellophane (such as saran wrap) can be used to seal in moister and keep the seeds at a reasonable temperature. Within just a few days, you should see the seeds beginning to sprout. This is the most direct way to begin, but some may prefer to test the seeds out, outside of the soil, first.

- A moist towel or sponge. Another option is to test out the seeds before planting them in the soil. You can place a group of seeds onto damp paper towels, or put them into the holes of a damp sponge. It's important to remember damp instead of wet. While some of the seeds will begin to change within just one day, others may take multiple days. Give it at least a week, and once the seeds start to crack open, you can place them in soil, following the instructions above.

- Using a mother plant instead of seeds. Other growers may want to forgo the seed process altogether, and instead, use clippings from a "mother plant". A mother plant is an adult plant which clippings of small branches can be taken from and replanted into soil. This is ideal for people who already know someone who grows and is willing to share their strain. This takes the hassle out of figuring out which seeds will work and worrying about germination.

It's a general rule of thumb that plants with longer vegetative periods will turn into larger plats and have greater outputs when they reach the flowering stage. Usually a minimum of two and a maximum of six weeks of this state are used and may grow up to twice or thrice their size. Male plants are usually cut down by gardeners since they don't give any buds and also have been known to contaminate nearby female plants with their seeds.

Most people who enjoy marijuana prefer to have as few seeds as possible. Part of the appeal of growing indoor is being able to reduce the chances of seeds, whereas outdoors, it's harder to prevent.

Female seeds are very sought after by indoor gardeners because they get rid of the risk of male plants, for the most part. If male buds do appear toward the end of the female plant's cycle of flowering, don't worry, just get rid of them. Young male flowers will not be able to contaminate the mature female, especially if you eliminate them quickly.

Chapter 3: Selecting Lights for the Plants

It almost goes without saying that without light, you won't be able to grow plants inside! If you look at each nation where marijuana grows wild, you will notice that the places are often very sunny. In these countries, the amount of sunlight and the amount of time the growing season is naturally allowed will result in gigantic plants that resemble trees more than bushes.

In many parts of the Northern parts of America, though, there is not enough sunlight in the right climatic conditions to produce the same quality or sized plants that grow in tropical countries or parts of South America. The answer to this problem, of course, is to take matters into our own hands and creating our own light source while growing cannabis indoors.

Less is more, in the beginning stages of seedling growth:

Many will claim that when it comes to weed growing, the more light the plants get, the better off they will be. In the very beginning stages of their life, however, the baby seeds don't require too much light and will be perfectly happy with low intensities, as far away as three feed from a HPS light. When using fluorescent lights, you should keep the plants closer to the lamp(s).

When growing indoors and using artificial light instead of sunlight, the lamps typically must be kept on during the entire day (or 18 to 24 hour periods). During these early stages, the baby seeds are in a vegetative growth stage, meaning that they will continue sprouting branches, leaves, and roots, but not buds, yet.

Eventually, you will want to reduce the amount of light to just 12 hours a day, as the plant transitions into the phase of flowering. This phase typically needs anywhere from two months to 10 weeks, although these specifications differ depending on the strain you use.

This is the time period where the female flowers start to grow and you get the first glimpse of the beautiful buds you will be enjoying later. In this phase, your plants will get much bulkier and will start to need and absorb more nutrition along with bright lights. Some gardeners like to use supplemental light to get the most out of their harvests.

Near the end of this process, you will want to cut down your plant and dry your buds. Some gardeners like to go through this process when they notice that the trichomes of the plant change from clear to a more cloudy color (to notice this, you will need a strong scope or magnifying glass), but as a grower becomes more experienced, they will develop their own tested, tried and true methods for knowing when to harvest.

Often times, the plants will have orange or red hairs growing from them when they are ready to be clipped, but some people prefer bud that was harvested late. The beauty of being your own gardener means that you decide!

As mentioned earlier in the book, you can use different types of light to effectively grow cannabis. There are many different types of artificial light sources and each does something different to your plants.

Why you shouldn't use regular light bulbs for growing cannabis:

The more common light bulb (incandescent) releases some frequencies that will be useful to the plant, but isn't the ideal light sources since it also has a high amount of infrared frequencies. These infrared frequencies will not contribute to nice leaves or flowers, but will instead make the growth be concentrated to the stem of the plant, making it relatively useless. This will result in the plant trying to stretch up to the light source and eventually becoming so skinny and tall that it cannot support its own weight and topples over weakly.

There are many different bulb brands to choose from. One is the plant spotlight that is still incandescent but puts off more blue and red light than the average household light bulb. This is an improvement from the typical light bulb, but has its downsides. For example, it emits a lot of head and can't be placed too closely to the plants. As a result of this, the plants will have to reach upward again and has the same danger of getting too tall and weak and toppling over. Red bands in the light appear to encourage growth of the plant stems, which is not ideal for getting a quality harvest. The goal here is to encourage growth of the foliage, not the steps.

Gro-Lux lights:

Gro-Lux lights are pretty popular when it comes to selecting fluorescent lights for plants, and possibly the most common brand of all, for home growers. This is because they are an effective and efficient choice. You can select anywhere from one foot to eight feet in light length, allowing you to start your garden in a small space (like a closet) or a large one (like a warehouse). This versatility makes this brand an obvious choice. There are two different options for selecting a Gro-Lux light:

- The standard option. This option gives you everything you need to grow high quality marijuana plants. Red and blue bands of infrared light will be emitted from the lamps, which your plants need to sprout thick and beautiful foliage and stay strong.

- The wide spectrum option. This choice emits the same bands of light rays that the standard offers, but plants need the blue and red bands to grow, which the standard allows for. This option releases infrared light, which has an unwanted effect on the stems, as mentioned earlier.

These options can also be used in combination with each other, but you cannot use the wide spectrum light by itself, since they were created to be used as supplementary light and are not as quality as standard grow lights. If you want to grow more than just a few plants, and intend to have a large operation, it might be helpful to know that typical fluorescent fixtures and lights (which are used in lighting for commercial purposes) can be great in combination with the standard Gro-Lux option I went over above.

These lights, known as "cool whites", are the most affordable of all, typically. They give off the same amount of blue light as the standard Gro-Lux option, which is necessary for growth of foliage in the plants.

Intensity levels of Gro-Lux lights:

Both the wide spectrum and the standard lamps reviewed above come in a few different intensities. They are Very high, high, and regular. It's possible to get a nice group of plants going under just the standard, regular lamps, and enjoy your results quite a lot. The main difference between using the high or very high options is the amount of time needed for the grow operation. With the very high intensity option, plants will grow three times faster than they would with standard lights. In fact, it isn't uncommon for people to end up with a plant that is up to four feet high in just eight weeks using one of these high intensity lights.

With very high intensity lights, it may be necessary to raise the lamps each day, which translates to a two inch per day growth rate. One downside to this option is affordability, and you get what you pay for with this. The very high output fixtures and lamps cost nearly twice as much as the standard option. If you are willing to spend the money, you won't be disappointed, and the money is well worth what you get for it.

Once you have selected your lights, you will probably want to know how much light your plants will need each day. The date that your plants will reach their fully matured state depends on how much light you give them. The longer the period of darkness on your plants each day, the quicker they will start blooming. In general, it's better to have less darkness during the first half year of the life of your plants. The more mature your plants are before they begin blooming and seeding, the better quality marijuana you will end up with when it's time to harvest. After the plant has bloomed, it has a slowed metabolic rate which will mean that the quality of the plant does not increase as it gets older, at least not to the degree that it did when it was younger and hadn't bloomed yet.

This means that you should allow your plants to get as old as you can before letting it mature so that you will get the highest level of potency possible when you harvest your buds. One great way to make sure your plants don't bloom until you want them to is to keep the lamps on at all times. Eventually, a plant will start blooming.

Some general guidelines for lights:

- If a plant gets 12 hours of light each day, the maturation period can be expected to occur within 2 to 2 and a half months.

- If a plant gets 16 hours of light each day, you can expect to see them bloom within 3 and a half to 4 months.

- If a plant gets 18 hours of light each day, you will see booming in 4 and a half to 5 months.

It's recommended that you put your lamps on a timing system to make sure that the hours of light they are receiving each day is consistent. You can find these at hardware stores. Look for a vacation timer, which is intended to make it appear as though people are home during the day when they go out of town, to prevent robberies. This can be hooked up to your grow lights to make sure your plants get constant light and darkness amounts.

Chapter 4: Soil and Fertilizer

Once you have picked out your seeds and lights, it's time to select some high quality soil. You need to find the best kind you can get, because opting for cheap, lower quality options will only make you waste more money in the long run. Great soil means that you will get a high yield with amazing quality in the shortest amount of time possible, and what gardener doesn't want that? Don't use non-sterilized options for soil, because you will more than likely discover parasites in it, and then it will be too late to save your plants. You can search for great quality soil at a nearby plant nursery, gardening shop, or even certain grocery chains.

When selecting soil, make sure it has the following properties:

- Created for optimal draining: Your ideal soil choice should contain extra properties for draining such as pearlite, sponge rock, or sand.

- Optimal pH levels: Look for soil that has between 6 and a half and 7 and a half pH levels, since marijuana doesn't like acidic soil.

- Moisture and nutrient retaining properties: Look for soil that contains humus, this will help the soil stay healthy, moist, and nutritious for your plants.

It is possible to use any dirt you found, even in your back yard, but then you will need to put it through a sterilizing process, which makes it not worth the hassle. Just spend a bit of extra money and get some quality soil, your plants and you will thank yourself later!

What to look for in fertilizer for your cannabis plants:

Once you've selected the right soil to use, you can start focusing on fertilizer. Cannabis is typically a hungry plant which enjoys a lot of food, but don't get too carried away with this. If you're new to gardening, you may be tempted to over-fertilize your plants in hopes of creating strong and beautiful harvests, but this can be damaging to the roots and plant.

If you select a quality soil, as advised above, it should contain enough nutrition to sustain the young plants for at least three weeks, which means you don't have worry about fertilizer until after this period. What you should remember is that you should gradually, and not suddenly, introduce fertilizer to your plants. Begin with a diluted concentration of the fertilizer and work your way up over time. There are multiple quality fertilizers available out there, and two of the best are Eco-Gro and Rapid-Gro.

- Ego-Grow: This is great for marijuana plants because it contains special properties that prevcent soil from becoming too acidic, which we mentioned earlier is not good for the plants.

- Rapid-Gro: This option has been used in cannabis growing for quite some time and can be found in most of America.

Most fertilizers available on the market change the pH quality of the soil. This means that adding, to your soil, fertilizer will raise the acidity of the soil. Over time, the fertilizers will break down in the soil and increase the amount of salt, making it acidic and possibly harmful. Eventually, the leaves will start turning brown due to too much acid.

It's good to keep in mind, also, that as plants age, the roots are less efficient at transferring nutrients to the leaves. You need to make sure you prevent these salts from accumulating in the soil and ensure that your plant is receiving its needed nutrients. Dissolve your chosen fertilizer in lukewarm water and place in a spray bottle. This mixture can be sprayed directly on the plants, allowing the leaves to soak up all of the nutrients.

You can put fertilizer directly into the soil in addition to feeding the leaves, but again, be sure you aren't overdoing it. Keep in mind that you should gradually increase the amount you are feeding your plants. Cannabis appears to be able to handle as much food as you'd like to give it, bearing in mind that it needs to be gradually introduced over periods of time, instead of all at once.

In the first few months or growing, feed your marijuana plants every three days or so. The growth rate of the foliage will slow down as the plant prepares to bloom and begin producing seeds, which means that, at this time, the nutrient intake of the plants should slow down. Don't ever feed your plants right before you plan to harvest since doing this will increase production of foliage but decrease THC.

Containers for your soil and plants:

Once you've decided on the right soil and fertilizer to use, you will need to select containers for your baby plants. Your chosen containers should be clean and sterile, particularly if they are used. Small steps like this can be the difference between a wonderful harvest and a failed garden, so take your time and be careful.

Which size container you choose will directly impact how fast the plant grows and what size it reaches. You should transplant the young plants as little as possible, since this process can shock the system of the marijuana and it will have to take time to recover. During this recovery period, the plant may stop growing, which will only slow down your operation.

Here are some guidelines for containers for your plants:

- Your first containers should be six inches or less, and ideally made of plastic or clay material.

- When transplanting, get the larger container ready by having it full of soil with a small hole scooped out in the center. Flip the plant upside down, including the pot, and tap its edges on a hard surface like a table or counter. This should make the root ball and soil come out easily, while retaining its shape. It's important to keep this as intact as possible.

- Use Jiffy-Pots, if you want to make the whole transplanting process much easier. These are created using peat moss which can be placed directly into soil, decomposing and then letting the system of roots pass easily right through the walls.

- For your second containers, make sure you get a size of three gallons or more, since cannabis plants hate to have cramped space for their roots.

- Always make sure your containers are large enough for the roots to spread out and flourish, otherwise your plants will suffer.

Chapter 5: Temperature and Ventilation

Since marijuana evolved to grow in specific conditions, it's important to pay attention to the temperature and humidity of your grow room. The most perfect temperature for light is anywhere from 68 to 28 F. For your plants' hours of darkness, you need to make sure they are getting a temperature drop of at least 15 degrees.

Pay attention to the moisture in the room:

Try to have your gardening room dry. Since you are ideally wanting plants that have a nice sticky coating on them, the plant needs to be convinced that it must develop that coating to protect itself from drying out. If the room is too human, the plants will not develop this resinous protection which growers seek. If the room is too hot and dry, however, the plants will start turning brown.

Be sure to instate proper ventilation in your grow room:

Making sure you have the right ventilation in your plant room is quite important, especially for bigger gardens. It is not as much of a concern if you only have a plant or two, but the more you have, the more necessary proper ventilating is. Plants filter poisons out through their leaves and use them to breathe, so not having a room properly ventilated could cause the plants to die. Free motion of air in the room manes that the plants will stay healthy because they can breathe.

For small grow operations (like a closet-sized one), just opening the door every so often will create enough free movement of air for your cannabis plants. Here are some other tips to keep in mind when considering air flow for your cannabis plants.

Breathe around your plants often: It's also worth noting that spending time around your plants aids their growth because of the carbon dioxide you emit when you breathe.

- Consider a fan: If you have a grow room in a room like the basement or attic where stale air tends to accumulate, a fan is a great addition to your garden. This mimics the movement of wind that is present when cannabis grows outside naturally, which will help the plants develop stronger stems.

- Think about a dehumidifier: If your grow operation was started with the intention of getting your buds nice and sticky, a dehumidifier is your friend. This is because it helps to create a hot, dry environment for your plants which will encourage them to create that protective resin mentioned earlier in the book. These aren't a very cheap purchase, however, and you can expect to pay at least $100 on one, so only make this choice if you are serious about your marijuana and not just trying it as a one time thing.

Chapter 6: Watering

The most ideal situation for a grower would be living close to a fresh, clean, and natural water source. However, most of us live in cities and our water sources tend to be full of chemicals that natural water sources don't have. Most of these chemicals, us humans have adapted to over time, since we've been ingesting them most of our lives. Your marijuana plants, however, haven't had time to adjust to this unnatural change, and need clean, fresh water. Quality water means quality plants.

Letting the water you use on your plants stand before using it:

It's advised that before you water your plants, you allow the water to sit in a non-sealed container for a day or two before using it. There are a couple of benefits to this.

Eliminates chlorine: If you absolutely have to use city tap water, let it sit out in an open container for at least 24 hours so the chlorine has a chance to evaporate from it and can't infect your fragile plant friends. If the chlorine levels in the water are very high, anti-chlorine drops can help you. These can be purchased at your local pet or fish store.

It allows the water to get to room temp: Pouring cold water on your plants can shock them and cause issues. It's better to have a neutral temperature for the water.

It's important that when you're watering your cannabis garden, you're doing it correctly, and that means being thorough. If you have your plants in containers of at least three gallons, you can water them using up to three quarts of fresh water. The point behind this is making sure the soil is moisturized evenly and that the water reaches all the way down. If you only use a small amount of water, it can't go very far down into the dirt, meaning that the thirsty roots underneath the moistened soil will have to start turning upward to reach the water.

The importance of quality drainage:

Another important aspect of watering is making sure your plants have proper drainage. Find containers that have holes in the bottom to release extra water that the soil doesn't need. This is important, because without a drainage system, extra water can accumulate and the roots of your plants can rot. Excess water can also cause mildew in the pots of other soil issues. Your soil must allow for water to evenly be distributed throughout it without becoming packed or hard.

As mentioned earlier, make sure your soil has pearlite or sand and you should have no issues with draining it. If you're unsure of when is the best time to water your plants, feel the dirt with your fingertip. If the soil still feels somewhat damp, it's okay to wait a day or even two. The topsoil will be drier naturally than the soil underneath. It's possible to over-water your plant, which is arguably worse than too much dryness. Marijuana in its natural habitat is more likely to handle a dry spell than it is to survive too much water or a flood. It's quite simple; give your plants water when they need it and be thorough, and don't give them any when they aren't in need.

Chapter 7: Things to Watch Out

Growing plants indoors is arguably safer than outdoor operations, but there are still a few dangers that can occur. The main issue is bugs. You want to avoid this problem at all costs, because once your precious cannabis crop gets infested, the problem will likely stay.

To avoid this issue, you must:

Use quality, sterilized soil and clean containers. If you go with unsterilized soil, you run the risk of bugs or insect eggs already being inside of the soil. It was mentioned earlier, but it's worth saying again, make sure you sterilize your pots and containers, especially if they have been used before!

Don't bring other types of plants into the grow room. Your grow room should be reserved strictly for cannabis. Bringing other types of plants in means you run the risk of insects from those plants getting onto your marijuana and ruining it. It's not worth the risk.

Don't allow pets near your garden. Animals carry insects, so if you have a dog or cat, make sure it's never allowed into your grow closet or grow room.

Inspect your plants often for signs of bugs. The faster you catch this issue, the better chance your garden has of recovering, so make sure you are examining the plants regularly for signs of insects. This includes unusual spots, drooping branches, and holes or browning on the leaves. Look underneath the leaves as well as on top of them. It's worth investing in a magnifying glass for this process, so all of your time and money doesn't go to waste.

The possibility of needing insecticide:

These measures should protect your plants from bugs, but if you find yourself with an issue despite all of this, you will need to get some insecticide. The first sign of bugs is depressed and sick looking plants. Mites steal the leaves' enzymes which makes the color go dull and sometimes brown. You might see tiny black insect eggs on the plants.

Finding a safe insecticide is easy with a quick Internet search. Even after spraying, you need to continue to examine your plants regularly. All it takes is one bug laying eggs on your plants and they will be re-infested.

Chapter 8: Pruning the Plants

Some gardeners don't bother pruning their plants, because it isn't absolutely necessary. However, it does improve the quality of your plants. The first reason for this is that it allows for something called secondary growth, which makes the plants thicker. It also will allow more light to reach the less mature leaves of the plant. A few stray strands of your plants may grow naturally bushy and thick if they don't get pruned, the sap will move right up to the top of the bush where the flower will be thickest and most coated in resin.

It's also possible that your plants will grow spindly and tall for how old they are at just a few weeks, which would mean they need some extra trimming to encourage a full nice leafy bush. Just a few weeks into the life of your plant, it should have a minimum of two branch sets and at least four clusters of leaves at the top.

Instructions for pruning your cannabis plants:

When you are pruning your plant, all you need to do is cut the top off near the place with the two branches are opposite to one another. You can use a box cutter or regular razor blade to make a straight slice.

Using the pruned branches as clones. If you desire, you may use these clippings as clones and place them in water, wait for roots to grow, and then plant them in soil, letting it make another marijuana plant. If you plan to do this, make sure you slice off the end of the clipping once more, but this time do a diagonal cut rather than straight so more of the plant gets exposed to the rooting solution and water it gets placed in.

The great part about taking clippings from your garden is that more tops will be produced. The top part of the plant has the most resin which means that's where THC is concentrated, which is what most growers are after.

Every time you remove the top of a branch, your plant will put out at least two more at the base of where you cut. For this reason, many choose to partake in pruning. Doing this also allows the lower branches to grow more quickly than they would if they were just left alone. Although it develop better, a cannabis plant that has been pruned does not produce more flowers every time than a plant that hasn't been pruned.

If you decide to prune your plant, you should keep these tips and facts in mind at all times:

As mentioned earlier, every time you cut a tip of a branch, the stem splits and makes even more. Compare it to humans getting haircuts every so often in order to have healthier hair that grows better.

Pruning is recommended because it allows for your growing plants to get their uneven branches under control, without causing harm to the plant.

Make sure you don't clip the growing tops of young plants until after the vegetative state has started, which will be apparent by the five bladed leaves having started to form.

Some gardeners prune their plants after only a month to aid the growth of the lower parts of the plant which don't typically get as much access to light, due to being blocked from the upper branches. These clippings will quickly make sure the horizontal spaces get filled in.

The most potent part of your marijuana plants is in the top of the plant, and once at least three months have passed since they started growing, you should actually be able to cut these and begin enjoying your plant's output.

It's possible to prune the tips at nearly any stage of the plant's life (except for the very beginning), but be sure you aren't doing it too often. Too much pruning is very bad for your cannabis plants.

Don't start haphazardly pruning your plants without any preparation. You must have a system worked out and be sure that you have thoroughly researched the right way to do this. This book should give you the basics, but watching videos online can also be a helpful way to make sure you're doing it right.

Your plant needs time to recover in between pruning. Every time you slice off the tip of a branch, it needs a few days before it can start growing again in that particular place. The rate at which this new growth can occur depends on the strain you're growing as well as the quality of the growing environment.

It's preferable and recommended that you do your pruning mostly in the earlier stages of your plants' lives, rather than while they are flowering or getting into the vegetative state.

Try to do your pruning in the mornings instead of the evenings, so your plants have the rest of the day to recover and heal from the clipping. Do not prune every time a new node develops, instead, give the plant time to heal and only clip every second or third one.

Allow time for a new node to appear before you begin pruning the branch. Give it time to reach at least a few millimeters beyond the previous growth's new leaves.

It's preferred that you use a razor blade or small scissors. Don't use your hands if you can help it.

If you notice that your plants are looking sick or unhealthy, hold off on pruning. Although the tips you clip can be smoked, this should not be the reason you do it.

You may be tempted to cut the buds off the female plants as they begin to flower, but you will severely limit the end product of your harvest if you give in to this temptation.

Indica plants are usually smaller and bushier than Sativa plants which means they won't need pruning as often.

Do not ever clip more than one growing portion from any branch on your plants.

Focus on the taller branches of your plants when you prune, since this makes sure that the branches underneath can grow upwards to form an area that is wider and more reachable for your light sources.

When you clip, be sure to let the fluid that appears stay there. It exists to help the plant heal itself and recover.

Removing dried leaves from the plant will help its growing process, but try to leave the healthy leaves alone as much as possible.

Most gardeners would like to grow marijuana without seeds. To do this, you need to get rid of male plants right when you discover them, by cutting the main stalk right over the soil.

Chapter 9: Harvesting and Curing

Now that you have successfully grown your plants, you are probably itching to get it into a usable state! The best way to know for sure when your plants are ready to be clipped is finding images online of what the plants will appear like when they are ready. Curing it properly is important for having the most enjoyable experience with the marijuana you worked so hard to grow. There are a couple of things to keep in mind when you're ready to harvest your crops.

Uprooting your finished plants:

You will need to pull the plant up by its roots and let it hang upside down for a full day. Then you will put each uprooted plant into a paper bag for a few days, leaving the bag open so the buds can dry. You will know when they are dried by how they feel when you touch them. They should be dry, which signals that they are done and ready to be used however you wish.

Stripping the leaves and storing them:

Next you will remove the leaves from the stalk and put them into a sealable jar. The main danger at this stage is mold, so make sure they are not packed too tightly so air can reach them. Check on this every day to avoid mold, which you will be able to sense by the smell of the leaves in the jar. If you do notice an acrid scent in the jar, you can spread the leaves out on paper to dry, which shouldn't take long.

Those are the simple instructions on enjoying your harvest. You can now choose which ways you want to enjoy your beautiful buds. You can, of course, smoke the buds once they are dry enough or even use them to make some canna-butter for edible marijuana treats.

Conclusion

Thank you again for purchasing this book!

I hope this book was able to help you feel prepared to begin your very own cannabis growing journey. Anyone can do it, it's just a matter of having the right information. This guide was created with the intention of equipping you with all you need to know to start growing your own indoor plants at home.

The next step is to follow the guidelines I gave you about selecting materials, setting up a grow space, and watching your plants grow! As a new gardener, you will learn a lot your first time around. If you decide to continue on with this pursuit of growing cannabis, you will notice that, each time, you are a bit wiser as to what works and what doesn't. After a few successful harvests, you will be a pro.

I wish you the best of luck in this pursuit and hope that my information was helpful to you.

Finally, if you enjoyed this book, then I'd like to ask you for a favor. Would you be kind enough to leave a review for this book on Amazon? It'd be greatly appreciated!

Thank you and good luck!

Made in United States
North Haven, CT
07 December 2022

28092956R00030